Network Marketing Mindset

Personal Development and Confidence Building for Network Marketers

www.networkmarketingkingdom.com

Table of Contents

Introduction

Chapter 1: Believe in yourself and in your business

Chapter 2: How to stay motivated

Chapter 3: How to deal with rejection

Chapter 4: How to have confidence and attract people

Chapter 5: Vision board and affirmations

Chapter 6: Take action now

Conclusion

Bonus Video: How To Get Leads and Customers Online

Subscribe To Get Free Tips On How To Generate Leads and Get Customers

When you subscribe to get network marketing tips via email, you will get free access to exclusive subscriber-only resources. All you have to do is enter your email address to the right to get instant access.

These resources will help you get more out of your business – to be able to reach your goals, have more motivation, be at your best, and live the life you've always dreamed of. I'm always adding new resources, which you will be notified of as a subscriber. These will help you get an endless amount of leads and customers.

Visit
www.networkmarketingkingdom.com/video
to Access The Bonus Video

Introduction

I want to thank you and congratulate you for reading the book, *"Network Marketing Mindset: Personal Development and Confidence Building for Network Marketers"*.

This book contains proven steps and strategies on how to deal with the daily rejection in the network marketing profession.

Network marketing is by far the most difficult industry to learn and stay encouraged in.

Many people quit because they don't have the leadership skills and confidence to stick it out.

Daily rejection from recruits and leads can be very destructive to your confidence.

It's nice to say "so what, who's next" when people hurt your feelings. Trying to recruit can cause a lot of difficulties when it comes to friendships and relationships.

If you don't learn the right skills, it's possible that you can alienate people to the point where they don't want to be around you, because they think you're going to try and recruit them.

Network marketing itself has a bad rep to a lot of people not in the industry, they may think the opportunity you're offering them is a pyramid scheme or a scam.

If you're working the business, this constant rejection can take a lot out of you. It will leave you wondering if it's the right thing for you.

In this book, I will go into why network marketing isn't for everyone and ways you can have leads come to you instead of you chasing them.

Also, how to become a better person overall. How to live a better and more fulfilled life.

How to never give up on your dreams of financial freedom and continue on your journey to network marketing success.

Let's be honest-- network marketing is a people business. You're going to get your feelings involved.

This business is built on not just your effort, but the effort your team puts in.

That's why you constantly have to focus on making yourself a better person. Like attracts like.

So if you become more confident and get your mindset right you and your team will become unstoppable.

With these simple strategies, you will learn how to make this your best business and your best life.

Thanks again for reading *Network Marketing Mindset*, I hope you enjoy it!

Chapter 1: Believe In Yourself and Your Business

Believing in yourself sounds easy, but it's one of the hardest things to do. This is because today there is so much competition and it seems like you'll never get a piece of the pie.

But what you have to realize is, there's always going to be someone better than you at something.

Don't ever waste your time trying to compare yourself to others. It's okay to model them in order to strive for what they have, but it's never okay to compare yourself.

You don't know what it took to achieve what they have. Maybe they have more time than you, maybe they don't have any kids, maybe they work 15 hour days, you just never know.

Don't compare their situation to yours. You also don't know how long they've been doing what they're doing.

When you look at successful network marketers, you don't see the late nights, the studying, and skill building it took for them to get to where they are.

They may have poured hundreds and thousands of dollars into their education. You just don't know-- so don't compare.

To believe in yourself you have to learn to stop comparing yourself and start working on yourself.

You can start by asking yourself the most important question: "Is network marketing right for me?"

Network marketing does have a ton of benefits but

realize that it's a people business and you have to depend on people in order to make money.

Also, realize you don't have a lot of control of your business, your company can change the compensation plan at any time.

But one thing does remain the same, you can earn as much as you want. There is not a cap. Also, the start up cost is low, and you gain confidence by interacting with others.

There are many pros and cons, but are you down for whatever is yet to come? Are you willing to deal with people quitting and your company changing its policies?

If so, you believe in your business and the business model.

If you can get past the negatives you can move forward.

Do you believe in yourself? Do you believe you have what it takes to be successful in life?

If not, what's holding you back?

If you're reading this book you need encouragement. Daily!

Start taking your mindset seriously. Do what it takes to start thinking and acting like someone of value.

You can start believing in yourself by accomplishing something. Set a goal to recruit at least one person by next week.

If you achieve this goal, your belief will skyrocket.

But you need more than a goal, you need a plan.

Start investing in books and courses about network

marketing. Take yourself seriously and your business seriously.

Once you learn the skills your confidence will increase.

Get yourself organized. Stop playing games, and get out there and do the best you can with what you have!

Don't let anyone tell you you're not good enough. Ignore the people who tell you that this business isn't worth doing.

Ignore the people who aren't on the same track as you. It's time to let go of some of those relationships that are dragging you down. And you know which ones I'm talking about.

You're only as good as you feel. Start taking better care of your body.

Be the best you. Wake up early and go to sleep late.

Having success is going to take sacrifice.

This means no T.V. (especially the news), no video games, no senseless spending, no vacations.

If you truly want to reach your goals, give up some of the things that are wasting your time.

Become more of a productive person.

Start saying yes to the things that will make you a better person. Like seminars, working out, and eating healthy.

Get out of your comfort zone and start being more serious and disciplined.

Chapter 2: How To Stay Motivated

One of the hardest things to do in any business is to stay motivated. Although we want to go full time and quit our jobs, we often time lack the discipline to do so.

The great thing about this is we do want more. We know we have a way to go full time if we work hard and stay committed.

But getting there is the struggle. To wake up every morning ready to work is not normal, as human beings, we have mental blocks that at times hold us back from success.

We want to be better and reach our full potential. We want to make that last phone call to that prospect. And we definitely want to be the best upline in the world, but we fall short mainly because of our beliefs.

Many times we don't take action because we don't know what we should be doing.

Daily Routine

In order to stay motivated, you need a daily routine. This is something that you will do NO MATTER WHAT. This is the thing that will allow you to plant seeds that will grow and come back to you for years to come.

The first thing to do is decide how many hours a day you want to work your business. Keep in mind that this is something you will be doing every single day with no days off.

I think three hours a day is a reasonable amount for

anyone. Rather you're full time or part time you can squeeze in three hours a day to build your business.

Of course, you can adjust it to make it more hours, but the thing we are going to practice here is consistency.

Your daily routine should be something that you do every day to grow your business and should include income producing activities.

To create your daily routine find what income producing activities you need to do every day to grow your business.

Once you've found them write them on a piece of paper. Then you need to separate these activities into timed tasks.

For example: Follow-up with prospects (1 hour)

However many hours you gave yourself (remember 3 or more hours) for your daily routine, make sure all your income producing activities will get done in the allotted time.

Income Producing Activities

If you're not focused on income producing activities, it can lower your motivation because you won't be seeing any results.

Also, knowing that you're working on income producing activities daily will increase your confidence.

The income producing activities in network marketing are:

1. Showing your presentation to as many prospects as possible

2. Talking to people about your opportunity

3. Following up with leads

4. Training your team to show presentation, talk people about the opportunity, and to follow up

So if you want to create a daily routine, these activities should be included in them.

Example:

Daily Routine (every day): 3 hours
-30 min show presentation to 2 people
-30min talk to 5 people about my opportunity
-1 hour follow up with leads
-1-hour team training

Whatever works best for you and your schedule, and of course you can up a number of hours and time spent on these different tasks.

Setting Goals

Goal setting is another way to stay motivated. Have you ever heard of SMART goals?

S- Specific
M- Measurable
A- Achievable
R-Relevant & Realistic
T- Time Bound

This is a checklist that you can use to make sure you're setting goals.

Having goals allows you to feel refreshed and motivated each month. Monthly goals work best to stay motivated.

Make sure your goals are not result oriented, so you won't get depressed. What I mean by that is make sure they don't focus on results because if you don't get that result, you'll feel like you failed.

Focus on action steps that you can take to achieve your goals instead.

For example, instead of setting a goal to recruit 10 people in a month. Set a goal to reach out to 10 people a day.

Your consistent effort with income producing activities will bring you results. There is no need to put yourself in a situation where you can't control the outcome.

Network marketing is based on people, you can't control any outcome. You cannot control what people do. You also cannot control what changes your company makes.

Therefore, a SMART Goal for your business might be: I will easily show my presentation to 60 people by 00/00/00 <== enter date here).

Have at least 3 goals for the month and make sure to keep them in plain sight. You can use things like a big white board or a note by your computer. Make sure to read them every day to stay motivated and focused.

Envision The Life You Want

You may lack motivation because you're not sure what type of lifestyle you want to live. What type of lifestyle would make your life must fulfilled and happy?

Start by doing an exercise where you close your eyes and envision how you truly want your life to be. From the time you wake up and the time you go to sleep.

If time and money were not a problem, what would you do with your day?

Be very specific. What type of car do you want to drive,

what would your house look like? What would you do with your family?

Write down your dream life. Keep this close and refer back to it whenever you need a pick me up.

If you really want to speed things up, read this when you wake up and before you go to bed.

Your Why

Knowing why you do what you do will help you to get out of bed in the morning and get to work.

If you know your purpose for living, and you are sure of everything you're working towards-- then you're well on your way to financial freedom.

Is your why to help others start their own business? Helping others to start their own business can be a life changer. Even if they don't stick with network marketing and decide to go in a different direction, think of the impact it can have on their life.

You offering them an opportunity to see that they can run a business may help them realize that there's a better life for them and that they have what it takes to be successful.

Accountability Partner

Find an accountability partner that you can work with weekly to discuss your progress and your goals.

Hold each other accountable for everything you're working toward. Your accountability partner should be someone who is like-minded and motivated like you.

They don't have to be in network marketing, but they should be an entrepreneur so you two can relate.

Mastermind

Join a mastermind group for network marketing. This is a place to share your ideas and progress with others.

This will keep you motivated and inspired when you see others getting results.

There are many free groups on Facebook and others that cost. Find one that's right for you and that you'll benefit from.

Make sure not to just read what's in the group but to stay active and participate.

If you can't' seem to find one that's right for you, start your own.

Events

Events are always a motivator. They make you get your off your butt and into the mood to take action right away.

Events work so well because you get exposed to the many people who are doing well-- that means this is possible for you.

It makes you want to be the next one on stage. Therefore, you take massive action!

Attend network marketing events, your company events and meetings, business seminars, etc.

Commitment

To stay motivated in your company, you have to be committed. This means doing things even when you don't feel like it.

This means taking action even when you're uncomfortable.

Commitment means staying up until it's finished, not going to sleep when you're tired.

It means answering your team members call for the 3rd time in the row that day.

It means being a person of your word and following up.

Make a decision today to be committed to your goals and your dreams and motivation won't be a factor.

Habits

Develop habits that other successful network marketers have. Habits go right along with discipline.

By creating habits, you'll find yourself doing what you need to do without having to fight with procrastination.

You'll start to do things without having to think twice; to the point where if you don't do it, you won't feel right.

The best way to develop a habit is to start off small. For example: Challenge yourself to wake up at 5am every single day. As you create these small habits, they will turn into big successes.

Research shows that you shouldn't try to form more than three habits at one time. So pick three small habits right now that you want to start implementing starting tomorrow. Tell yourself that you'll stick with them for at least a month.

Chapter 3: How To Deal With Rejection

Rejection is something that is going to happen in this business. You cannot escape it, you will hear the word "no", or even worse.

You may sometimes ask yourself if it's worth it, well... that's for you to decide. If your ultimate goal is financial freedom, there are many business models that are more rejection free.

But I'm assuming since you've purchased this book that you're in network marketing for more than the business model-- it's because you want more than money.

You want others to see you successful, you want to build confidence, you want to meet like-minded people, and you want to change people lives.

You chose to do this. Everything you wake up and do is a choice and an investment.

People are going to be rude, they are going to laugh at you, and they are going to tell you that you can't make money doing this.

Let their disbelief be the reason that you make it to the top! Do not allow people to decide rather or not you will be successful.

Use that as fuel to make tons of money and have fun doing it.

But the truth is you'll never truly get over being rejected, it's something you deal with.

Rejection will make you stronger, and it can either make you or break you.

If you use rejection as fuel you will make it. If you use it and let it get to you – you will end up giving up.

If you ever leave the network marketing profession, do it on your own terms, not because of something someone said.

It's natural for people to be skeptical about things they have no idea about. Also, you don't know their story-- and this profession isn't right for everyone.

Just be yourself and reach out. You're giving them an opportunity to better their lives-- they can take it or leave it.

It's not you that they don't trust, it's the business or business in general.

Many people are afraid, and it takes a few exposures for people to really feel that this may be something they want to commit to.

Try first to build trust and rapport with leads instead of telling them to just join your team or buy from you.

Remember that it's all about the numbers. Many will join you, many will leave you, but it's only a few you need to gain success.

Don't be afraid to ask, and don't be afraid to get rejected.

This is why I recommend daily motivation and daily action. Make sure your mind is right before you talk to anyone.

Your mindset is what determines your earning potential. Feed your mind what it needs daily and you will do what you have to.

You only live once, so decide now to live a fearless life of freedom.

And make sure to do something, keep busy. The more you think, the less you'll make. If you find yourself thinking too much, you may get depressed. Your mind is a tricky thing that wants you to remain comfortable.

Implement things right away, stay busy, and only fill your mind with positive things.

Chapter 4: How To Have Confidence and Attract People

Confidence is not something you're born with. It's something you must work on every day-- just like motivation.

Confidence building is not simple and it takes dedication and a "can do" attitude.

If your "why" is big enough, and you have goals set for yourself; your confidence levels should have already increased.

We are confident in the things we know work. So if you're constantly putting in the work by being committed to your daily routine then you are well on your way.

Confidence comes from within but the way we feel and look physically can also play a huge role.

Encouragement

Gain confidence through encouragement and support of other network marketers and team members.

Also, remember that your team members need encouragement and recognition constantly in order to feel appreciated.

Keep yourself around encouraging people that are want to see you make it.

Read personal development books and quotes that uplift your spirit.

Do your best to stay encouraged and watch your

confidence soar.

Health

You only feel as good as you look. Take great care of yourself. We all know the things we should do, but taking care of our health can be a struggle sometimes.

It takes dedication and will power to truly become healthy.

But what is your health worth to you? When you do better you feel better.

This means exercise, eating right, and drinking plenty of water.

Your health is an investment. What's the point of making all this money in network marketing if you won't be around to enjoy it?

Style

Everyone has their own style. The way you dress may be increasing or decreasing your confidence.

Believe me, I'd rather make a million bucks than look like a million bucks-- but you look how you feel.

What can you wear that will make you feel more confident in yourself?

If you don't own it, maybe it's time you invest in yourself.

Attraction Marketing

I don't know if you've ever heard, but attraction marketing is the new way of network marketing.

This is when you're not asking people to join your team, but people are coming to you.

This is when people are calling you and buying from you because something about you that they're at attracted to.

To succeed at attraction marketing you have to be the "go to person" in your company or in the network marketing industry in general.

Once people see you as an expert, they will be attracted to you and want to join your team.

To be the go-to person, make sure that the material you learn you share with others.

No one is born an expert, we all had to learn from someone.

Really start studying network marketing and be a wealth of knowledge and share what you know.

This is what attraction marketing is all about. Wanting to be that person or be near that person because of the value you've provided for them.

When you help someone or you seem to be the go-to person-- everyone will swing your way.

Chapter 5: Vision Board and Affirmations

These two strategies are ones that will allow you to have a more productive and positive mindset, which in turn will allow you to bring success into your life.

Vision Board

A vision board is a board that is dedicated to what you want to see your life look like in the future.

All you have to do is get a poster board, magazines, tape, and scissors.

Get magazines that are geared toward what you want your life to be like.

The best ones are travel magazines.

Cut out words and pictures of things you want to come into your life.

The idea here is to envision what you want your life to be like. This is an opportunity for you to learn more about yourself.

Below is a picture of my vision board for this year, just to give you some ideas.

You can have all images or all words, it's up to you. Just make it your own and make it true to your heart.

Merge your goals and the vision for your life into your vision board and you're good to go.

Hang this in a place where you'll see it every day. Such as an office or living area. Look at it any chance you get. You'll find over time all these things will come true for you.

Affirmations

Affirmations are uplifting phrases about yourself that will be repeated out loud until you change your mindset.

Your mind will believe things that you tell it.

We want to fill our minds with things that we want to bring into our lives.

Make a list of things that may not be true, but you want

to come true. For example, some of mines are:

- I am beautiful

- I am confident

- I am in a top earner in my company

- I am intelligent

- I am a great wife, sister, and daughter

- I am successful

- I am financially free

- I sponsor people effortlessly

- I vacation once a month

- I have free time to do whatever

- I am a multimillionaire

- I change people's lives for the better

- I am an action taker

- I own my own dream house and car

- I am a speaker and author

So what do you want to be? Write down your list or put it in your phone, somewhere where you'll have access to it.

Read your affirmations in the mirror every single day when you wake up and before you go to bed.

Look yourself in the eyes, this is you changing.

Chapter 6: Take Action Now

So enough talking, let's get to work. You learned how to set goals and stay motivated.

No longer allow your mindset to get in your way. Get uncomfortable-- this means you're growing.

Listen to plenty of audio that will feed your brain with the right stuff. Sometimes motivational music will even do the trick.

Do whatever it takes. Be committed and ever give up!

Always be reading the latest books on network marketing and take all the training you can to learn the industry.

Remember that in to attract people, you must share what you know and what you have learned.

Apply what you learned immediately. Keep investing in yourself and your dreams.

Constantly watch YouTube videos that are motivational and uplifting.

Keep learning and never stop growing.

Refer to your goals daily. Work toward your goals daily by doing you daily routine.

Constantly refer to your affirmations every morning and every night.

You have what it takes to be successful and it's always been in you. Once you realize you're good enough you will prosper.

Learning is great. Many of your competitors are still in

the learning stage. Only a small percentage take action.

Be the one that takes action. Be the doer! Be an inspiration to yourself, your team, and your family.

When people think of you, they should think of success, hard work, and commitment.

Today is better than any to get started. For as long as you live, it's ever too late to change.

Conclusion

Thank you again for reading *Network Marketing Mindset*!

I hope this book was able to help you to gain confidence and grow your business.

The next step is to get started mapping out your goals for the month and find an accountability partner.

Finally, if you enjoyed this book, then I'd like to ask you for a favor, would you be kind enough to leave a review for this book on Amazon? It'd be greatly appreciated!

By leaving a review, you'll help others to find the book. It will also give me feedback on what I can improve, and what I've done well.

Thank you and good luck!

Preview of 'Internet Marketing For Network Marketers'

Chapter 1: Website Creation Strategy

Creating a website is the first thing you'll need to do in order to take your business online. If you truly want to create a business that works 24/7, no matter if you're there are not, you will need a website.

Creating a website is actually quite simple, but it's the upkeep and consistency that will determine your success in the end.

Just like building a company offline, online will take work-- maybe, even more, work. But that's just in the beginning.

By setting up a website to bring you leads all day, you will be ahead of most people in the industry.

To get even further ahead, you will need to constantly add valuable content to your website which will, in turn, help build your team or get you more customers.

What Will Your Website Be About

As a network marketer, your website's subject will depend on what you're trying to do. Would you like to generate leads or customers?

You can always go back and create another website, but for now think about what you want to focus on.

The thing about success is you have to focus. What is the one thing that will bring you closer to your goal right now?

Is it having customers so you can have "right now money" and share the results which in turn will help to bring in more recruits?

Or is it bringing in more recruits, which in turn will define you as a leader and attract even more recruits?

Creating A Website To Get Customers

Building a website to generate customers will be simple but you need to know some basic things.

Do not use your company's name on your website. This is for two reasons: 1) it's most likely against your company's guidelines 2) You want to brand yourself in order to build trust with the leads that come in.

On this website, you'll be creating content that has to do with your company's products. For example, if your company sells shoes. You want to create pages that help people with making shoe selections, finding the right shoe, finding quality shoes, etc.

All your content on your website will be centered around one subject.

This is called a "niche site". A niche site is when you focus on one particular subject and create content around it.

If your content is valuable and helps the customer out, they will want to buy from you. This is when you can send them over to your company website where they'll make their purchases. More on this later.

Creating A Website To Get Recruits

Creating a site for recruits will be similar to creating a website for customers.

Again, make sure not to mention your company's name. You will be branding yourself.

Branding yourself is when you're using your name and not your company's name while providing value through your website content.

You don't want to mention your company's name because they are already branded. You want leads to join your team because of you.

Anyone can join a company, people will only stick around if they see you as a person that can help them get what they want.

You'll be creating content that helps other network markers. Think about the problems other network marketers just like you are having and solve them.

Once you do this you will create trust and be looked at as the "go to person" for network marketing.

In turn, they will either want to join your team or buy any information products and training you may have. More on information product creation later.

There is also an alternative for this if you truly want more targeted leads. You can create a website that is focused on helping people in your particular company.

So when people search for more information about your company, you will have a site that has all the information they were looking for.

Leads will feel they have an advantage by joining your team because the content you've created for them is valuable and you look like you know what you're doing.

Why You Shouldn't Create A Website For Free

There are many sites out there like blogger.com and wordpress.com that allow you to set up an account and create a website for free.

I'm against these types of sites for many reasons.

The first reason is professionalism. Creating a website that ends with .wordpress or .blogger will look unprofessional.

People will take you and your business more seriously when you use a domain name that ends in .com

Also, if you go with those free sites you will not own your content. Whoever hosts your site will.

You also won't be able to monetize it the way you want to. Many of those sites have restrictions against things such as affiliate links and your own ads.

If you're not serious, and you're just dabbling in network marketing then you can create one of these websites. Just keep in mind that you will be giving up all control.

There are many benefits to using trustworthy hosting companies. You get customer support and you can create unlimited websites. This means you won't have to buy more hosting in order to create another site.

How To Create A Website

Now we're going to go into how to create an actual website. If you already own a website or blog you can move onto the next section.

Domain Name Rules

A domain name is the web address you type into a browser in order to get to a website. For example: Google.com is a domain name.

There are a few rules you need to follow when naming your website.

5. Your domain name should have relevant keywords on what your site will be about

6. Avoid using your company name

7. Make sure to use .com

8. Avoid using dashes

9. Should be short and easy to remember

Registering A Domain Name

If you buy hosting first, sometimes you'll be able to get a free domain name with the host you choose.

I buy all my domain names from Godaddy because it allows for all of them to be in one place. You'll learn more about why you may want more than one domain name in later chapters.

Also, if you ever want to switch your hosting for any reason, you will not have to worry about transferring your domain name.

Transferring a domain name from one host to another can take up to three months.

To avoid all of this just register your domain name with Godaddy so if you ever want to change your host or use the domain name for something else you can easily just go in and do it.

Register your domain name in Godaddy by going to www.Godaddy.com and typing in the domain name you came up with of in the search box. Make sure to use the guidelines mentioned above.

If your first possible domain name is taken think of another one, keep trying until you find one that sounds right, looks right and works for you.

Make sure you buy a .com because this is the most universal ending for domain names and you will not encounter any trouble if using this.

Tip: To get the best price on your domain name search Google for "Godaddy Promo Codes"

Set Up Hosting

Next, you need to decide who you want to host your website. There are many options to go with. There are a ton of hosts you can use.

Find out which is best for you, make sure first that the host offers a platform that you can easily set up WordPress.

I use a company called Bluehost. To buy hosting with them go to Bluehost.com. I recommend them because they have outstanding customer service and you can easily set up WordPress.

After finding a host, install WordPress and you're good to go.

***For a complete tutorial on how to set up your website visit www.networkmarketingkingdom.com/website ***

The Website Creation Strategy

Now that you've registered your domain, you've set up WordPress, you're ready to start creating content.

The content you create is what will constantly bring leads into your funnel so you can turn them into customers and recruits.

The goal here is to create content related to your particular product if you're trying to reach customers, or your knowledge of the industry if you're trying to get recruits.

Really find your niche. For example: If your product is related to makeup you can create a website with content about makeup tips, tutorials, product reviews, etc.

Avoid using your company name. Before you create any pages make sure you use Google Keywords Tool to find keywords to use in your pages that are not too high in competition and now too low.

There are also paid tools that can help with your keyword research and find keywords that people are searching for. This may be worth it if you want to do in-depth research or find keywords and competition.

This will allow your site to rank in Google. Use search engine optimization (SEO) to get found for different words and phrases so you can drive traffic to your site.

My favorite WordPress plugin to use for this is WordPress SEO Yoast. SEO Yoast shows you how to optimize your pages and posts for the search engines.

As you can see, internet marketing is a huge learning curve. There is so much to learn, it is a lot of work.

Your website's keywords are only one way you will get traffic to your website, though. You will also get traffic from email and social media marketing. More on that later.

Traffic is very important. There are tons of ways to get traffic and you want to expose your site to as many people possible.

The equation is simple. More traffic=More leads.

The thing that will make you successful at creating a website that stands out is you have to create content for a very targeted audience. The content you create has to teach someone how to do something.

When teaching others how to do something, make sure if they follow your blueprint that they'll get results.

After getting results from using your free content, they'll become raving fans and buy any product or service you have to offer in the future.

Raise your standards when it comes to creating your content. Do the research that is necessary and don't be lazy about it.

If you truly put your all into your website you will stick out from all the other marketers trying to do the exact same thing. In turn, people will become attracted to you because you will be known as an expert in whatever you're teaching about.

The websites that do best are the ones that teach someone how to do something.

Keep in mind that you can easily create more than one website. If you use a host that allows you to have unlimited domains, you can create lots of websites and only pay for hosting once a year. To create a new site all you'd have to do is buy a new domain name.

So you'll be able to create sites for recruiting, getting customers, and possibly one for your team.

As long as you're creating lots of content that is valuable and use the proper keywords, you will generate traffic.

You may be wondering why I don't suggest you create a

blog. This is because a blog will constantly have to be updated.

You want a static website that allows you to create something once and leaves everything else up to the automated system.

So make sure the content you create is evergreen and not about events or subjects that are time dependent. If you create content that is not evergreen you can use it in your social media updates.

Creating A Team Site

Creating a team site is the best way to leverage your time. If you put out valuable content on another website or through other channels such as social media or email then people will want to join your team.

People will also want to join your team once they see your professionalism you have by having a dedicated team site. The best way to get more team members is to get results and share results. In turn, this will attract others and they'll want to do what you're doing.

Make your team site a membership site exclusive only for your team members. Here you can walk them step-by-step through the process after they sign up to join your team.

You can also offer them training and everything they need to be successful on your team.

This will allow you to leverage your time. You will not have to answer the same questions over and over again. If you put everything you would say to a new team member on that site you will save them time and you time.

Visit www.NetworkMarketingKingdom.com to check out

<u>the rest of Internet Marketing for Network Marketers</u>

Check Out My Other Books

Below you'll find some of my other popular books that are popular on Amazon and Kindle as well.
Alternatively, you can visit <u>my author page</u> on Amazon to see other work done by me.

<u>How To Get Customers In Your Network Marketing Company: The Complete Guide To Converting Leads Into Loyal Customers</u>

<u>Internet Marketing For Network Marketers: How To Create Automated Systems To Get Recruits And Customers Online</u>

<u>Network Marketing Selling Secrets: 50 Ways To Get New Customers</u>

Bonus Video: How To Get Leads and Customers Online

Subscribe To Get Free Tips On How To Generate Leads and Get Customers

When you subscribe to get network marketing tips via email, you will get free access to exclusive subscriber-only resources. All you have to do is enter your email address to the right to get instant access.

These resources will help you get more out of your business – to be able to reach your goals, have more motivation, be at your best, and live the life you've always dreamed of. I'm always adding new resources, which you will be notified of as a subscriber. These will help you get an endless amount of leads and customers.

Visit
www.networkmarketingkingdom.com/video
to Access The Bonus Video

www.ingramcontent.com/pod-product-compliance
Lightning Source LLC
Chambersburg PA
CBHW071018180526
45168CB00003B/1475